Colophon

©Mathias Jansson (2025)

"Return of the Pixel in Contemporary Art"

ISBN: 978-91-86915-84-1

Published by:

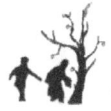"jag behöver inget förlag"

c/o Mathias Jansson

Tvärvägen 23

232 52 Åkarp

SWEDEN

http://mathiasjansson72.blogspot.se/

Print: Lulu.com

Disclaimer: This book is written with help of ChatGPT. The author has previously conducted extensive research on the subject and has also contributed texts about Game Art and Pixel Art in different journals. The essays have been improved, edited and proofread by the author before publishing.

Contents

Introduction 3

Chapter 1 – Prehistoric Pixels and the Modern Grid 5

Chapter 2 – From Pixels to Polygons: The Evolution of Video Games 7

Chapter 3 – The Pixel Returns 11

Chapter 4 – The Pixel on Screen: From CRT Glow to LCD Sharpness 15

Chapter 5 – Art Games: A New Medium 18

Chapter 6 – 8-Bit Video Games on the Art Scene 27

Chapter 7 – The Pixel Goes Offline 38

Chapter 8 – Takashi Murakami: Pixel Flowers and the NFT Revival 44

Chapter 9 – The Pixel Today: Subculture and the AI Horizon 48

Introduction

In the early 1980s, the pixel was not an aesthetic choice—it was a technical limitation. Home computers and early game consoles could only render a handful of colors and blocky shapes. Yet out of these restrictions grew an entire visual culture. The 8-bit era produced iconic imagery: the chunky sprites of *Space Invaders*, the brightly colored worlds of *Super Mario Bros.*, and the labyrinthine dungeons of early RPGs. For a generation, these pixels defined what digital imagination looked like.

As computer graphics advanced, the industry moved quickly toward realism. By the late 1990s and early 2000s, video games and digital media strove to eliminate the pixel, replacing its rough edges with smooth surfaces, detailed textures, and cinematic visuals. The pixel seemed destined to become a relic of the past, a symbol of obsolete technology.

But in recent decades, something unexpected has happened. The pixel has returned—not as a technical necessity, but as a deliberate artistic strategy. In popular culture, games like *Minecraft* and platforms like *Roblox* embrace blocky, low-resolution aesthetics, turning simplicity into a new form of creative power. In contemporary art, a new generation of artists, many of whom were born long after the 8-bit era, are rediscovering pixel aesthetics and transforming them into tools of expression. They build interactive installations, machinima, digital paintings, and virtual worlds that reference, remix, and reinvent the language of the pixel.

This book traces that journey: from the pixel as the foundation of digital graphics in the 1980s, through the decades-long pursuit of hyperrealism, to its surprising revival in the hands of contemporary artists today. It asks why the pixel—a unit once seen as primitive—has become so meaningful in our present moment. Is it nostalgia? Is it technocritique? Or is the pixel, in its stark abstraction, a timeless visual form that continues to inspire imagination?

By weaving together the history of home computing, the evolution of video games, and the practices of today's digital artists, this book explores how the pixel has shifted from constraint to concept, from technological limit to aesthetic choice. The pixel has returned—and with it, a renewed way of seeing, playing, and making art.

Chapter 1 – Prehistoric Pixels and the Modern Grid

The idea of the pixel—or small units that make up an image—long existed before computers. Roman mosaics are an early example: tiny cubes of stone, glass, or ceramic, called tesserae, were placed together to form images. Each cube worked like a pixel, and the colors and arrangement of many cubes created the final picture. This method of building complex images from small pieces is a key idea that continues in modern and digital art.

Modern artists took this idea in new directions. Josef Albers' *Homage to the Square* series (1950s–1970s) uses simple nested squares of color to explore how colors interact. Piet Mondrian's paintings simplify forms into lines and colored blocks, creating precise, modular structures.

Kazimir Malevich's geometric works, such as *Suprematist Composition: White on White* (1918), use squares, circles, and rectangles on neutral backgrounds. Each shape is a visual unit that interacts with others, creating rhythm and balance. Malevich combined intuition with careful planning to make these compositions, similar to how pixels work in a digital image.

Gerhard Richter's paintings *Color Charts* series (1960s–1970s) is made of grids of colored rectangles. He paints them carefully, sometimes using chance, creating patterns that feel both organized and lively.

The individual blocks of color function like pixels, showing how small units can create big visual effects.

Gerhard Richter's stained glass window in Cologne Cathedral, unveiled in 2007, stands as a striking fusion of contemporary art and Gothic architecture. Measuring 106 square meters, it comprises 11,263 hand-blown glass squares, each 9.6 cm^2, arranged in a grid of 72 colors. This design draws inspiration from Richter's 1974 painting *4096 Farben*, a systematic grid of color permutations, translating the concept into a monumental architectural form. You can also see Richter's stained glass window as a work of pixel art.

Art historian Rosalind Krauss, in her 1979 essay *Grids*, argued that the grid is a defining structure of modern art. She described it as a tool that allows artists to organize space, focus on formal relationships, and explore abstraction systematically. In Krauss' view, the grid represents a break from illusionistic representation and narrative, emphasizing autonomy, order, and conceptual rigor. Within the context of pixel and video game aesthetics, Krauss' insights highlight how modular units—whether squares in a painting, tesserae in mosaics, or digital pixels—can structure both perception and meaning. The grid becomes a visual and intellectual framework, linking historical practices of modular composition to contemporary digital and interactive art.

Chapter 2 – From Pixels to Polygons: The Evolution of Video Games

In the late 1970s and early 1980s, a quiet revolution began in living rooms and bedrooms around the world. For the first time, home computers and video game consoles brought interactive digital images into everyday life. These machines were limited in power and memory, but they unlocked a new way of seeing, playing, and imagining. At their core was the pixel—tiny squares of light that became the building blocks of an entire generation's cultural imagination.

The Age of 8-Bit

The early home computers—the Commodore 64, ZX Spectrum, Atari 800, and later the Nintendo Entertainment System—operated on what is now called "8-bit" architecture. In practice, this meant extreme limitations. Screens could display only a handful of colors. Sprites, the small moving images used for characters and objects, were blocky and abstract. Backgrounds were built from repeating tiles. Yet these constraints did not stifle creativity—they shaped it.

Games like *Space Invaders* (1978), *Pac-Man* (1980), and *Super Mario Bros.* (1985) turned pixels into icons. A yellow circle with a wedge missing became a ravenous creature. A plumber made of a few dozen colored squares became the face of an empire. Children did not see the crude geometry—they saw characters, worlds, and adventures. Their imaginations filled the gaps, transforming flickering pixels into living stories.

The 8-bit era did more than entertain. It taught a generation the grammar of digital culture. Players learned to navigate virtual spaces, to interpret abstract symbols as meaningful environments. Just as the book once taught people to read language, the video game taught them to read pixels.

From Play to Possibility

As home computers spread, they became more than just machines for consumption. Many users, especially children and teenagers, learned to program their own games. Magazines printed lines of code that readers could type in, customize, and experiment with. For the first time, digital creation was accessible at home. A young player could imagine a game, write the code, and see it appear on screen. This was not only entertainment—it was empowerment.

The pixel thus carried a double meaning. It was both the symbol of digital play and the entry point into digital creativity. The children of the 1980s became the first generation to grow up inside digital culture.

The March Toward Realism

As technology advanced through the 1990s and 2000s, developers pursued a dream: to make games look more like the real world. With the introduction of 16-bit and 32-bit systems, pixels grew smaller and more detailed. Soon, 3D graphics arrived, and polygons replaced sprites. Games like *Doom* (1993), *Final Fantasy VII* (1997), and *Half-Life* (1998) marked the transition to immersive, cinematic experiences.

By the early 2000s, the race toward realism accelerated. Textures became photorealistic, characters expressive, worlds vast and detailed. Today, the latest blockbuster titles boast hyperreal graphics powered by advanced rendering engines, ray tracing, and AI-driven animations. The pixel has not disappeared—every digital image is still made of pixels—but its presence has been smoothed away, hidden under layers of realism.

A Generation Transformed

For those who grew up with early video games, the pixel was more than a technical unit. It was a cultural touchstone. It shaped how they saw images, how they told stories, and how they understood technology. Video games did not only change entertainment—they changed a generation's relationship to media, imagination, and identity.

The children of the 1980s and 1990s became artists, designers, programmers, and thinkers who carried the pixel with them into adulthood. Some embraced the march toward realism, working in industries that sought to erase the blockiness of the past. Others looked back, rediscovering the simplicity and symbolic power of the pixel.

What began as a limitation has become an aesthetic, a language, and a memory. The evolution from 8-bit sprites to hyperrealism is not just a story of technological progress. It is also a cultural journey—one that continues to shape the art and media of today.

Chapter 3 – The Pixel Returns

By the early 2000s, the relentless march toward realism had created a paradox. As video games became visually spectacular, players began to look back fondly on the blocky graphics of their childhood. The pixel, once dismissed as primitive, now carried emotional weight. It became a symbol of simpler times, a shorthand for an era when play was direct, imaginative, and unmediated by cinematic ambition.

This cultural longing—often described as *technostalgia*—was not simply about missing the past. It was about reinterpreting the visual codes of early computing and gaming in a new cultural context. Pixel art became a form of retro chic, appearing not only in games but also in fashion, advertising, and contemporary art.

Indie Games and the 8-Bit Revival

A crucial force in the return of the pixel was the rise of indie games. Freed from the demands of blockbuster production values, independent developers embraced pixel aesthetics both as a practical solution and as a conscious artistic strategy.

Games like *Cave Story* (2004), *Braid* (2008), and *Fez* (2012) used low-resolution graphics not because of technical necessity, but because of their cultural resonance. These games demonstrated that players craved more than realism—they craved style, atmosphere, and ideas. The pixel provided a visual shorthand that connected audiences to gaming's roots while enabling new forms of storytelling.

The "8-bit revival" was not merely nostalgic. It was also experimental. Developers twisted and reimagined the pixel, using it to explore themes of memory, loss, identity, and technology. What began as homage soon became innovation.

Nostalgia as Cultural Currency

Nostalgia itself became a marketable commodity. Retro-style games were sold as authentic experiences, promising players not only entertainment but also a return to the emotional landscapes of their youth. The pixel, once invisible, became a brand.

Yet nostalgia was not only commercial—it was also critical. Many artists and designers used pixel aesthetics to comment on the passage of time, on how digital culture ages, and on the fragility of memory in an era of constant technological obsolescence. The pixel became a metaphor for cultural memory itself: fragile, imperfect, and yet enduring.

Block Worlds and Social Play

While indie games revived the 2D pixel, another development expanded the pixel into three dimensions. *Minecraft* (2009) and later *Roblox* (2006, with explosive growth in the 2010s) transformed blocky aesthetics into immersive, social environments.

In these platforms, the pixel evolved into the voxel—a three-dimensional cube that functions like a pixel in space. Players used these building blocks to construct elaborate worlds, share them with others, and even design their own games. The blocky aesthetic was not a limitation but a liberation: it made creation accessible to millions of players who could build without advanced design skills.

Minecraft in particular became a cultural phenomenon, bridging generations and inspiring educational projects, art installations, and even architectural experiments. The block world was not simply nostalgic—it was a new kind of canvas, one where social play and creativity fused together.

The Pixel as Building Block for Creativity

The return of the pixel was not about accuracy, but about imagination. A cube could be a house, a mountain, a sculpture, or a narrative device. Just as 8-bit sprites once invited players to fill in the gaps with imagination, voxel environments encouraged collective creativity.

The block became the democratic unit of digital culture. Everyone could play, build, and share, turning the act of creation into a form of social interaction. The pixel was no longer hidden—it was proudly visible, celebrated as the foundation of digital play and art.

Pixels as Language

As the pixel re-entered popular culture, artists began to reclaim it as a visual and conceptual language. Pixel art resurfaced in galleries and installations, not just as nostalgia, but as commentary.

Some artists embraced glitches—errors in digital rendering—as aesthetic forms. Others painted by hand in pixelated styles, bridging traditional and digital techniques. The pixel became a symbol of mediation, a reminder that all digital images are constructed.

Pixelation as Critique and Commentary

Pixelation also carried cultural and political weight. To pixelate an image often means to censor it, to obscure what cannot or should not be seen. Contemporary artists used pixelation to question surveillance, identity, and representation in the digital age.

By pixelating faces, bodies, or environments, they reminded viewers of the tension between visibility and invisibility in a world dominated by images. The pixel became both a shield and a mirror—an aesthetic that both hides and reveals.

The return of the pixel is not a simple story of nostalgia. It is a story of transformation. From indie games to global platforms, from retro graphics to critical art practices, the pixel has reemerged as a vital tool for creativity, memory, and commentary.

Chapter 4 – The Pixel on Screen: From CRT Glow to LCD Sharpness

When we speak of pixel art, we often imagine the same small, blocky units of color—but the way these pixels appear has changed dramatically depending on the screen technology. The difference between cathode-ray tube (CRT) displays of the 1980s–90s and today's liquid-crystal displays (LCDs) is not just technical, but aesthetic and cultural.

CRT Aesthetics: The Glow of the Pixel

On CRT screens, pixels were not fixed squares but glowing spots of light. Each was created by an electron beam striking phosphor, which produced a soft bloom around the dot. The result was a blended, luminous image where colors bled into one another. Game artists often designed with this softness in mind: dithering techniques (checkerboard color patterns) created the illusion of gradients, and jagged edges were smoothed by the glow of phosphors. The CRT thus became part of the artwork, completing the image in the player's eyes.

LCD Aesthetics: The Grid Revealed

By the early 2000s, CRTs gave way to LCD and LED screens. Here, pixels are hard-edged, uniform squares with no blending or glow. Every boundary is visible, turning what was once softened into a rigid grid. Classic games suddenly looked harsher, and some of their illusions broke down. What was designed to look "alive" and painterly appeared flat and mechanical.

At the same time, younger pixel artists embraced this sharpness. Rather than simulating the soft blur of CRTs, they leaned into the geometry and clarity of the pixel, celebrating its status as a modular building block of digital culture. This became central to what scholars and critics call the Pixel Renaissance of the late 2000s and 2010s, when indie games and contemporary artists revived 8-bit and 16-bit aesthetics in new cultural contexts.

Old School vs. New School Pixel Art

We might think of two "schools" of pixel art:

- **The CRT School (1980s–90s):** Pixel art as a practical solution to hardware limits, made with an understanding that screens would blur and blend images. The aesthetics were inseparable from the machine.

- **The LCD School (2000s–today):** Pixel art as a conscious, stylistic choice. No longer bound by necessity, artists reproduce the pixel look on sharp modern screens, using it as a language of nostalgia, minimalism, and cultural memory.

When the Pixel Renaissance emerged in indie games (*Cave Story*, 2004; *Fez*, 2012; *Undertale*, 2015) and in contemporary art, CRT screens were already disappearing. The new generation of artists and developers grew up with LCD as their normal screen—they never saw the softened glow of phosphors. So the shift from CRT to LCD redefined pixel art. What began as a blurred, glowing illusion tied to hardware became a crisp, mathematical language celebrated for its clarity and modularity. The old pixel school worked within the limits of technology, while the new pixel school embraces those limits as symbols, turning pixels into signs of memory, culture, and identity in the digital age.

Chapter 5 – Art Games: A New Medium

"Art games" are video games created primarily as artistic works rather than commercial entertainment. They often emphasize conceptual ideas, narrative experimentation, or emotional experience, rather than high scores or conventional gameplay.

The movement emerged in the early 2000s as a reaction to both mainstream gaming's pursuit of realism and the rise of independent development. Artists used digital game engines to create works that functioned as interactive art installations, exploring themes such as mortality, memory, identity, and social critique.

For the first generation of pixel artists—born in the 1970s—art games offered a medium to combine their childhood experiences of 8-bit games with experimental art practices. These artists began making art games roughly in the mid-2000s, after decades of immersion in video game culture and independent digital experimentation.

Jason Nelson's *Game, Game, Game and Again Game* (2007)

Jason Nelson, born in the early 1970s, is a digital poet and net artist. His games blend 8-bit aesthetics with experimental literature, turning interactive play into a poetic medium.

In *Game, Game, Game and Again Game* (2007), Nelson uses hand-drawn, low-resolution graphics reminiscent of early games. Players navigate surreal, glitch-like environments and encounter fragments of text, poetry, and absurd humor. The 8-bit-inspired visuals create a playful but unsettling rhythm, transforming nostalgia into a new poetic language.

Pippin Barr's *The Artist is Present* (2011

Pippin Barr, born in 1979, is known for stripped-down, minimalist games that mimic early digital aesthetics.

His art game *The Artist is Present* (2011) recreates Marina Abramović's MoMA performance as a low-resolution simulation. Players move blocky avatars through a gallery, eventually sitting across from a pixelated Abramović. The game questions both the translation of performance into digital space and the seriousness of art institutions.

Other works, such as *Let's Play: Ancient Greek Punishment* (2012), feature repetitive, unwinnable tasks in simple 8-bit style, combining irony, humor, and philosophical reflection. Barr demonstrates that pixel simplicity can be a tool for critique and experimentation, not just nostalgia.

Jason Rohrer's *Passage* (2007)

Jason Rohrer, born in 1977, treats game-making as an intimate form of artistic expression. His seminal art game *Passage* (2007) uses simple pixel graphics to guide a character through a narrow scrolling world, symbolizing the journey from youth to old age and death.

The blocky visuals are central to the emotional impact. They invite players to project meaning onto abstract forms, turning simple pixels into powerful metaphors for life, memory, and mortality. Later works such as *Gravitation* (2008) and *Between* (2009) continue this approach, using minimalist digital forms to explore human relationships and existential themes.

Daniel Benmergui's *Today I Die* (2008)

Today I Die (2008) is a short Flash-based art game created by Argentine designer Daniel Benmergui. Unlike traditional video games, it does not focus on winning or losing but on poetry, atmosphere, and transformation. The game presents a small, pixelated scene—a drowning figure in a dark ocean—accompanied by a line of text. By interacting with both the words and the imagery, players gradually shift the scene from despair to hope: changing words alters the world, light enters the sky, and the drowning figure finds new life.

Benmergui's use of lo-fi pixel graphics is essential to its impact. The simplicity of the visual style creates space for emotion and imagination, making the game feel like a digital poem. *Today I Die* became an important example of how small, experimental games could function as artworks, using the language of pixels and interactivity to explore existential themes of death, love, and renewal.

Carlo Zanni's *Average Shoveler* (2004)

Carlo Zanni, born in 1975, created *Average Shoveler* (2004) a browser-based game influenced by the graphic style of 1987's *Leisure Suit Larry*. The short game plunges you into a pixelated snowfall—each snowflake composed of live images from news, politics, sports, and entertainment feeds. As you shovel a path through the flurry, you clear not just a route but an information overload, temporarily ridding yourself of "the flurry of news" burdening your mind.

Average Shoveler merges pixel aesthetics, journalistic imagery, and interactive gameplay into an emotional metaphor for modern life. The task is Sisyphean: there's no victory—only the repetitive motion of clearing. As snowflakes burst and disappear, the game stages a poetic reflection on media saturation, mental clutter, and existential fatigue. The game's intent is not to entertain, but to provoke reflection. By using pixel-based mechanics, Zanni reframes low-res simplicity as a powerful tool for critique—examining information overload, the passage of time, and our relationship with digital media.

Jonathan "Cactus" Söderström's *Norrland* (2010

Jonathan "Cactus" Söderström's (b. 1985) *Norrland* (2010) is often cited as a raw and uncompromising example of the "art game" form. Known for his prolific output of experimental indie titles, Söderström—who later co-created the cult hit *Hotline Miami*—crafted *Norrland* as a pixelated exploration of boredom, violence, and isolation.

Set in the sparse landscapes of northern Sweden, the game confronts players with a series of unsettling mini-games: hunting, drinking, fighting, even acts of self-destruction. Its crude 8-bit style reinforces a sense of bleakness, echoing the aesthetics of early home computer games while subverting their playful innocence.

Instead of escapism, *Norrland* forces players to endure a monotonous and sometimes disturbing cycle of rural life, transforming gameplay into social commentary. As an "art game," it strips the medium down to its essentials—interaction, repetition, choice—then uses those mechanics to provoke reflection on alienation and human fragility. In doing so, Söderström demonstrates how lo-fi, pixel-based design can carry emotional and cultural weight far beyond nostalgia, positioning *Norrland* as one of many interesting experimental indie pixel art games from the time.

Olle Essvik's *Waiting For* (2008)

Another Swedish artist is Olle Essvik who created the interactive artwork *Waiting For*, an early example of a pixel-based art game. The work resembles a computer game but deliberately avoids conventional gameplay.

Instead, it functions like a theatrical performance where pre-programmed instructions are endlessly repeated in shifting order, producing a cycle without beginning or end.

The title alludes to Samuel Beckett's play *Waiting for Godot*, where nothing truly happens except the act of waiting. Similarly, *Waiting For* places the player in a loop of futility and anticipation, reflecting on time, repetition, and meaninglessness.

Though built in Flash technology (now obsolete), the game embodies the pixel aesthetic of the late 2000s, blurring the line between digital art, theatre, and gaming. Essvik's work demonstrates how the pixel can become a poetic medium for existential questions, far beyond its roots in video game entertainment.

Ian Bogost's *Guru Meditation* (2009)

Ian Bogost's *Guru Meditation* (2009) is a compelling example of how pixel art can be used to explore themes of stillness, patience, and the intersection of technology and spirituality. Developed for the Atari VCS and iPhone, the game draws inspiration from the Amiga computer's "Guru Meditation" error message, which was humorously linked to developers' attempts to meditate on the Joyboard peripheral during system crashes.

In *Guru Meditation*, players are tasked with sitting perfectly still on the Joyboard or holding the iPhone steady, embodying the practice of meditation. The game's pixelated visuals depict a yogi rising when the player remains motionless, symbolizing the attainment of zen. Time progresses subtly, with changing skies and ambient sounds, enhancing the meditative experience

Bogost's use of pixel art in *Guru Meditation* serves not only as an aesthetic choice but also as a medium to convey the game's themes. The simplicity and abstraction of pixel graphics mirror the clarity and focus sought in meditation, allowing players to engage with the game's message on a deeper level. This approach aligns with Bogost's broader exploration of "procedural rhetoric," where the rules and systems of a game communicate its underlying message.

Ian Bogost's *A Slow Year* (2010)

Ian Bogost's *A Slow Year* (2010) is a seminal work that reimagines the Atari 2600 as a platform for poetic expression. Dubbed a "game poem," it consists of four minimalist games—one for each season—that invite players into meditative, observational experiences rather than action or strategy. Each game is precisely 1 kilobyte in size, reflecting the constraints of early gaming hardware. The project also includes 1,024 machine-generated haiku and essays exploring the intersection of video games and poetry.

In the context of pixel art, *A Slow Year* exemplifies how retro aesthetics can be used to evoke introspection and temporal awareness. The game's deliberate pacing and simple visuals encourage players to slow down and engage with the passage of time, offering a contemplative alternative to the fast-paced nature of contemporary gaming.

The First Pixel Generation

What connects Jason Nelson, Pippin Barr, Jason Rohrer and other art games creators is their shared cultural inheritance. They were the first artists to grow up fully immersed in pixels, experiencing the formative years of 8-bit games and early home computing. Later, they transformed these childhood experiences into artistic practice, shaping what would become the first generation of pixel-based art.

For this generation, the pixel operates on multiple levels. As memory, it carries the nostalgia of childhood and the early culture of digital play. As experiment, it becomes a deliberate artistic strategy, using lo-fi graphics not out of necessity but as a tool for exploration. And as concept, it allows interactive digital forms to investigate identity, mortality, and broader cultural commentary.

Through their work, these artists elevated the pixel from a simple technological unit to a language of art— a medium for thinking about time, culture, play, and the digital experience itself.

This first generation laid the groundwork for subsequent artists and indie developers, who would adopt the pixel as a deliberate aesthetic and conceptual tool. Unlike Nelson, Barr, and Rohrer, many of these younger artists did not grow up with 8-bit graphics; they rediscover the pixel as a symbol of cultural memory rather than a lived experience.

For the first generation, however, the pixel was already home. It was a visual and conceptual vocabulary inherited from childhood, one that they shaped into the pioneering art games of the 21st century.

Chapter 6 – 8-Bit Video Games on the Art Scene

In the early 2000s, the art world began to recognize the creative potential of video games, giving rise to a new genre often called Game Art. Artists began using the aesthetics, mechanics, and interactivity of video games as a medium for artistic expression, exploring themes of history, memory, and digital culture. Among the pioneers of this movement were Feng Mengbo and Cory Arcangel, whose works illustrate how 8-bit video games could be reimagined as contemporary art.

Feng Mengbo: Long March: Restart (2008)

Feng Mengbo's (b. 1966) *Long March: Restart* (2008) is an immersive, large-scale installation that transforms viewers into participants. Players control a Red Army soldier navigating a side-scrolling landscape inspired by 1980s arcade games such as *Super Mario Bros.* and *Street Fighter*. Along the way, they confront pixelated enemies and collect power-ups, including Coca-Cola cans used as weapons—a playful yet satirical reference to consumer culture. The installation's life-sized projections and interactive gameplay blur the lines between spectator and participant, turning the art experience into a form of active engagement.

The project evolved from Feng's 1993 oil painting series, *Game Over: Long March*, into a fully interactive digital format by 2008. Its acquisition by MoMA in New York in 2010 marked a pivotal moment, signaling the art world's growing acceptance of video games as a legitimate artistic medium. Through *Long March: Restart*, Feng demonstrates how early game aesthetics can be combined with historical narrative to create work that is both visually engaging and conceptually rich.

Rafael Fajardo's *Crosser (2000)* and *La Migra (2001)*

Rafael Fajardo's *Crosser* and *La Migra* are compelling examples of how pixel aesthetics can engage with political issues. These hyper-pixelated games explore the U.S.–Mexico border crisis from opposing perspectives: one as a migrant attempting to cross, the other as border enforcement. By adopting the look and feel of vintage games such as *Frogger* and *Super Mario Bros.*, Fajardo draws on familiar gaming mechanics to create an approachable yet provocative interactive experience.

The games are deeply symbolic. In *Crosser*, players confront the dangers and uncertainties faced by migrants, navigating obstacles like desert terrain, rivers, and surveillance, highlighting the human costs of border policies. *La Migra*, by contrast, casts the player as border patrol, emphasizing the power structures and systemic enforcement mechanisms that shape the crisis. Together, they offer a dual perspective, fostering empathy and reflection on a politically charged subject.

In the context of Feng Mengbo's *Long March: Restart*, Fajardo's work shares a similar strategy: both artists employ pixel-based retro aesthetics to explore political or historical narratives. Mengbo reimagines Chinese revolutionary history as a side-scroller, turning ideological struggles into interactive play, while Fajardo uses the same language of early video games to humanize contemporary social conflicts. The pixelated visuals, far from being a limitation, function as a tool for abstraction and emotional engagement, allowing players to inhabit different roles and critically examine power, agency, and human experience.

Cory Arcangel: Super Mario Clouds (2002)

Cory Arcangel's (b. 1978) *Super Mario Clouds* (2002) is another landmark example of 8-bit video game art entering the gallery space. For this work, Arcangel took a 1985 NES cartridge of *Super Mario Bros.* and modified it to remove all elements except for the scrolling clouds in the background. The resulting installation presents pixelated clouds drifting across a blue sky, stripped of characters, obstacles, or soundtrack. By isolating these overlooked elements, Arcangel transforms a familiar game into a serene, contemplative visual experience.

The conceptual framework of *Super Mario Clouds* operates on multiple levels. By removing interactive components, Arcangel challenges traditional notions of gameplay, turning a dynamic game into a passive, reflective artwork. The piece evokes nostalgia for early gaming while commenting on the rapid evolution of digital technology and the ephemeral nature of digital media. As Arcangel noted, the work captures a sense of melancholy for those familiar with the original game, highlighting how omission and reduction can create emotional resonance.

First exhibited at the 2004 Whitney Biennial, *Super Mario Clouds* attracted widespread attention, underscoring the art world's growing interest in video games as both medium and subject. Its minimalism and conceptual clarity influenced subsequent generations of artists, encouraging exploration of interactivity, nostalgia, and the cultural significance of digital play.

Cory Arcangel: *I Shot Andy Warhol* (2002)

While his *Super Mario Clouds* (2002) became a landmark of early 8-bit game appropriation, another of Cory's significant works, *I Shot Andy Warhol* (2002), pushes the boundaries of video game modification as a conceptual and cultural critique.

The work is a modification of the classic Nintendo game Hogan's Alley (1984), originally a light-gun shooter where players had to fire at cardboard cutouts of criminals while avoiding innocent characters. In Arcangel's hacked version, the criminals have been replaced with images of Andy Warhol, while the "innocent" cutouts feature figures such as the Pope, Colonel Sanders, and Flavor Flav. Players are thus confronted with a surreal and provocative shooting gallery where art, religion, consumer culture, and celebrity collide in pixelated form.

By reprogramming a game from his childhood, Arcangel transforms a piece of entertainment into conceptual art that comments on pop culture, fame, and violence. The title of the work alludes to Valerie Solanas's attempted murder of Andy Warhol in 1968, linking video game violence to real-world art history and media spectacle.

Exhibited in galleries and museums, *I Shot Andy Warhol* demonstrates how early video game modifications could become platforms for critical reflection. Like much of Arcangel's work, it reveals how pixels—once thought of as trivial entertainment—can be used to question cultural myths, reframe history, and highlight the tensions between high art and mass media.

Anna Anthropy's *Dys4ia* (2012)

Anna Anthropy's work consistently intertwines personal narrative with game design, using the medium to explore identity, memory, and emotion. In nearly every piece she creates, she embeds aspects of her own life experience, inviting players into intimate, often vulnerable spaces. While not all of her games reach the raw autobiographical intensity of *Dys4ia* (2012) or *Queers in Love at the End of the World* (2013), these two works stand out as landmark examples of art games that confront issues of gender, sexuality, and selfhood.

Dys4ia offers a candid reflection on Anthropy's experiences with hormone replacement therapy, translating complex bodily and social experiences into simple, interactive sequences that evoke empathy and understanding. *Queers in Love at the End of the World* takes a different approach: a short, time-limited game in which players navigate a romantic encounter in a collapsing world. Its pixelated, minimalist aesthetic mirrors the fragility and immediacy of queer love, emphasizing fleeting moments of connection and intimacy.

In the context of art games about identity, Anthropy's work demonstrates how pixel-based interactive media can serve as a deeply personal and political canvas. Her games highlight how interactivity, narrative, and retro aesthetics combine to give voice to marginalized experiences, transforming play into an act of self-expression and social commentary.

Kristoffer Zetterstrand: Painting with Pixels

Swedish painter Kristoffer Zetterstrand (b.1973) merge classical painting traditions with the aesthetics of early computer graphics. Born into the era of home computers and 8-bit games, Zetterstrand grew up surrounded by the blocky visual language of the Commodore 64, Amiga, and Nintendo consoles. Instead of leaving this aesthetic behind, he carried it with him into his artistic career, treating the pixel not as a technological limitation but as a cultural building block.

Early Work: From Pixels to Paint

From the beginning of his career, Zetterstrand has used the pixel as a painterly device. His early works often combined references to Renaissance and Baroque art with the grid-like imagery of computer games, creating hybrid scenes where classical figures coexist with simplified, low-resolution backgrounds. By doing so, Zetterstrand positioned the pixel as part of art history, not merely digital ephemera.

His approach bridges two traditions: the Western canon of painting, with its emphasis on realism and depth, and the digital aesthetics of his youth, marked by flatness, grids, and vibrant blocks of color. The result is a unique visual language where oil painting and early computer graphics meet.

Minecraft and the Pixel as Medium

Zetterstrand's best-known contributions to contemporary digital art came through his collaboration with Markus "Notch" Persson, the creator of *Minecraft*. In 2010, Persson discovered Zetterstrand's pixel-based paintings online and invited him to create a set of artworks to be used within the game. These Minecraft paintings—low-resolution versions of Zetterstrand's real oil paintings—were integrated as in-game objects, decorating virtual homes and landscapes across millions of player-created worlds.

As part of Minecraft's *Tricky Trials* update, 20 new in-game paintings were added, 15 of them created by Kristoffer Zetterstrand and five by in-house artist Sarah Boeving, bringing the total number of artworks in the game to 46. Creating these digital paintings required more than just choosing colors and motifs—Zetterstrand also had to carefully consider the resolution and size of each work. Because Minecraft downscales paintings to fit the game's blocky surfaces, a misstep could turn a detailed composition into what he jokingly describes as a mess of JPEG artifacts.

To avoid this, Zetterstrand worked on his pieces almost like a pixel artist, manipulating images pixel by pixel to ensure that every block represented the intended visual and aesthetic effect. The smallest size paintings were omitted, a detail Zetterstrand was grateful for, as this would have added even more constraints to the creative process.

By translating pixels into paint, and paint back into pixels, Zetterstrand makes visible the feedback loop between art history, gaming culture, and digital life. His work shows that the pixel is more than just a technical artifact—it is a cultural lens, one through which we can explore the continuity between past and present, tradition and innovation, reality and simulation.

Invader: Pixel Street Art

Another example of an artist using pixel art is the French street artist Invader (b. 1969). Known for his mosaics inspired by the blocky characters of early arcade games like *Space Invaders* (1978), Invader brings the aesthetics of 8-bit graphics into public space. Using small ceramic tiles arranged like pixels, he installs these works illegally on walls across cities worldwide.

Invader's concept is to merge digital culture with the physical environment, turning urban space into a kind of giant video game. Each piece functions as both artwork and signature, a playful "invasion" that leaves traces of gaming nostalgia in everyday life.

To extend this idea, Invader documents each project as part of his global "invasions" and even developed an app, *FlashInvaders*, where users can "collect" his works like achievements in a game. In this way, his art transforms city streets into interactive, game-like experiences, demonstrating how the pixel has become a universal cultural language that bridges digital memory and contemporary art practice.

Hansaem Kim: *NOWON (2025)*

South Korean artist Hansaem Kim (b. 1990) is an example of new generation of artist inspired by 80s video games. Kim's work merges the aesthetics of early video games with contemporary digital techniques, creating installations that are immersive, playful, and conceptually sharp. Using pixelated imagery, glitch effects, and interactive screens, Kim constructs environments that invite viewers to step inside a virtual world while reflecting on memory, digital culture, and the nature of play. The work often references Japanese and Korean video game history, paying homage to the iconic pixel graphics of the 1980s while updating them for a 21st-century audience.

In 2025, Kim unveiled *NOWON*, an exhibition that bridges the gap between early digital gaming aesthetics and contemporary art. The title, "NOWON," carries a dual meaning: it refers to a real district in Seoul while simultaneously evoking the English phrase "No One Wins." This layered title symbolically reflects the artist's childhood memories and suggests a state in which no one emerges as a true "winner" within the endlessly repeating cycles of gameplay.

The exhibition featured a retro platformer game trailer created by the artist, along with three-dimensional works that combine digital drawings and 3D-printed sculptures. Kim's work merges the aesthetics of early video games with contemporary digital techniques, creating installations that are immersive, playful, and conceptually sharp.

Early 8-Bit Game Art: Legacy and Context

Feng Mengbo, Cory Arcangel, Kristoffer Zetterstrand, Invader and other artists demonstrate the creative potential of 8-bit video game aesthetics in contemporary art. These early works set the stage for a broader movement of video game-inspired art, paving the way for younger artists to explore the pixel not as a technological limitation but as a medium, a symbol, and a cultural language. By integrating gameplay, nostalgia, and interactivity, these pioneers established a precedent for considering video games as a legitimate and meaningful part of contemporary artistic practice.

Chapter 7 – The Pixel Goes Offline

Pixels were born as a practical necessity for early digital screens and video games. When most people think of pixel art, they imagine glowing screens, video games, or digital canvases. Yet in recent decades, artists have pushed the pixel far beyond its digital origins, transforming it into a sculptural, tactile, and conceptual language.

Artists increasingly explore pixel aesthetics in painting, sculpture, ceramics, and even public installations. Whether on canvas, in clay, or as part of interactive experiences, the pixel has become a universal unit of expression, connecting traditional media with contemporary digital culture.

Joo Jaebum: Masterpieces

Trained as an animator, the South Korean artist Joo Jaebum (b. 1983) discovered the expressive power of the pixel, not as a nostalgic gimmick but as a building block of contemporary visual culture. For him, the pixel is a unit that can carry memory, history, and emotion just as much as brushstrokes once did in painting.

In his series *Masterpieces*, Joo reinterprets works of art history—from Van Gogh's *Starry Night* to Pollock's splattered canvases—into simplified grids of colored squares. These pixel versions are not parodies but respectful homages, distilling the essence of famous paintings into their most elemental form. By doing so, Joo shows how the language of pixels can bridge centuries, connecting digital culture to the history of painting.

His practice extends far beyond the digital screen. In Tokyo he staged *Pixelized Adventure in Japan* (2023), a pop-up transforming game imagery into 3D sculptures, blurring the line between virtual and real. Joo's collaborations with brands such as Google, Nike, Dior, and Uniqlo have also helped bring pixel aesthetics into mainstream culture, showing their adaptability in both art and design.

Johnny Morant — Pixels Meet Old Masters

Among contemporary artists exploring the tension between traditional painting and digital symbols, Johnny Morant (b. 1982, Hong Kong; based in the UK) offers a compelling example of how pixel elements can interrogate and enrich classical imagery. A figurative painter trained in the UK, Morant specializes in oil paintings influenced by 17th-century masters, but with a contemporary twist.

He values intuitive brushwork—seeking to capture the viscosity of light and the fragile contours of form—but then subverts classical realism with the unblinking precision of pixels. As he explains: When reinterpreting … Old Master painting, I sometimes employ the most contemporary and ubiquitous mark in my arsenal—the pixel.

In exhibitions such as *Allegories of the Past, Present, and Future* and *Reinterpreting Baroque*, Morant's works confront viewers with this visual dialogue. His painting *The Raft of the Medusa, after Théodore Géricault* layers a classical composition with subtle pixel interjections, forcing us to reassess a familiar image through a contemporary lens.

Gustavo Viselner: *Game of Thrones*

Not all pixel art draws from art history or video game traditions; some artists turn instead to popular culture. Israeli artist Gustavo Viselner has gained attention for his series of digital illustrations that reimagine iconic moments from television shows and movies in a nostalgic 8-bit aesthetic. From *Game of Thrones* to *Friends* and *Breaking Bad*, his works transform beloved pop culture scenes into blocky, low-resolution images that evoke the look of early video games.

Viselner's art highlights how the pixel has become a universal cultural filter. By pixelating these stories, he both celebrates and critiques the way mass media is consumed in fragments, screenshots, and memes. His work demonstrates that the pixel is not only a tool for revisiting digital history but also a playful way to reinterpret the shared imagery of contemporary culture.

Toshiya Masuda: Pixel Ceramics

One striking example of offline pixel art is the work of Japanese ceramic artist Toshiya Masuda (b. 1977), who translates the flat 8-bit aesthetic into three-dimensional clay forms.

Masuda is best known for his series *Low Pixel CG*, where vases, sneakers, and other everyday objects are sculpted in ceramics but appear to be built from chunky cubes, as if lifted directly from an early computer game. Their surfaces are glazed to emphasize hard edges and block-like patterns, making them look digital even though they are handmade. This playful contradiction—the physical mimicking the virtual—forces the viewer to question the boundaries between real and digital craft. Masuda has said that he wants his art to "give a sense of discomfort and humor," highlighting how digital culture shapes our perception of material objects.

Hsu Tung Han – Pixelated Wood Sculptures

Taiwanese artist Hsu Tung Han (b. 1983) transforms traditional wood sculpture into a striking exploration of digital aesthetics. Known for his pixelated wood sculptures, Han carves figures and objects in solid wood—often human bodies, animals, or everyday items—then intentionally distorts portions of the forms into block-like, pixel-inspired shapes. This fusion of naturalistic carving and geometric fragmentation creates a tension between the organic and the digital, blurring the boundary between reality and virtual imagery.

Han works with high-quality materials such as walnut, teak, and Laotian fir, emphasizing the tactile and material presence of his sculptures while referencing the abstract simplicity of pixels. The resulting works often appear as if a digital image has been "glitched" into three dimensions, highlighting the visual and conceptual potential of translating pixel aesthetics into physical form.

By bringing the pixel into the real world, Han's sculptures encourage viewers to reconsider the interplay between the virtual and tangible, the precise and the organic, making him a interesting figure in the ongoing evolution of pixel art beyond screens.

Kristoffer Zetterstrand: Public Pixel Art Mosaics

Kristoffer Zetterstrand is a Swedish artist renowned for integrating pixel art aesthetics into large-scale public mosaics. His works often draw inspiration from early video games, blending digital culture with traditional mosaic techniques to create immersive public art installations.

One of his notable works is *Old School*, a series of seven glass mosaics commissioned by the Stockholm Art Council in 2007 and completed in 2008. Installed at Bromma Gymnasium in Stockholm, these mosaics depict pixelated representations of objects from vintage video games, celebrating the early days of digital gaming. The choice of glass as a medium adds depth and luminosity, enhancing the pixelated effect and inviting viewers to engage with the artwork from various perspectives.

Another significant project is *Erase to History*, a tile mosaic created for Vikingstad Skola in 2015, this work reflects Zetterstrand's interest in the intersection of history and digital imagery. The mosaic's design incorporates elements reminiscent of pixelated graphics, offering a contemporary interpretation of historical narratives.

Per Fhager: embroidered pixel

Per Fhager's embroidered pixel art offers a fascinating example of how traditional craftsmanship can reinterpret digital aesthetics. By transforming classic video game graphics into tactile, handcrafted artworks, he bridges the gap between digital nostalgia and artisanal practice. Using techniques such as Gobelin and cross-stitch, Fhager meticulously recreates the blocky, pixelated imagery of games like *Final Fantasy VI* and *Rainbow Islands*, adding depth, texture, and a physical presence absent in the original digital forms.

His work highlights the creative potential of limitations: both pixel art and embroidery rely on structured grids and deliberate use of space, turning simple units into expressive compositions. By reimagining digital images through a slow, manual process, Fhager underscores the enduring appeal of tangible art in an increasingly digital world, demonstrating how offline techniques can offer fresh perspectives on familiar digital forms.

Chapter 8 – Takashi Murakami: Pixel Flowers and the NFT Revival

The revival of pixel art in contemporary culture cannot be understood without looking at the rise of NFTs (non-fungible tokens) in the 2020s. While pixel art had long been celebrated in retro games, indie titles, and art installations, the NFT boom gave it a new cultural and economic significance. The pixel became not just a visual style but a symbol of digital scarcity and ownership.

Why Pixel Art Thrived in the NFT Era

The NFT space favored simplicity and clarity—artworks that could be easily recognized, reproduced, and circulated online. Pixel art, with its small file sizes, iconic shapes, and nostalgic references, proved perfectly suited to this new ecosystem. It bridged past and future: recalling the home computer revolution of the 1980s while embodying the cutting-edge of blockchain culture. Projects like CryptoPunks (2017) demonstrated how minimal 24×24-pixel portraits could become cultural icons and multimillion-dollar assets.

Pixel art thus gained a second life, not only as nostalgia but as a shared digital language—easy to replicate, easy to trade, and loaded with cultural meaning.

Murakami and the Pixel Revival

Against this backdrop, Takashi Murakami (b. 1962, Tokyo), founder of the *Superflat* movement, brought his own iconic motifs into the pixel-NFT arena. Murakami's work has always dissolved the boundary between high and low culture, mixing traditional Japanese art, anime, and consumer aesthetics. His smiling flower became a global brand, appearing in paintings, sculptures, and collaborations with Louis Vuitton and Kanye West.

In Murakami.Flowers (2021), he reimagined this flower motif as 24×24-pixel images, directly referencing early 8-bit game graphics. The project generated 11,664 unique variations, each one a tiny digital painting, recalling both the NES-era pixels of the 1980s and the modular logic of NFT collectibles.

Working at such a reduced scale forced Murakami to think like a pixel artist—carefully adjusting colors and shapes to avoid "JPEG artifacts" when downscaled, much like game designers of the past. In his words, the process meant painting pixel by pixel, a contemporary echo of early video game graphics.

NFTs as Cultural Playground

Murakami did not stop with *Flowers*. He collaborated with RTFKT Studios to create *Clone X avatars*, launched Flower Jet Coin NFTs tied to a exhibition in 2023, and released "108 Flowers Revised" NFT trading cards in 2025. These projects show how Murakami uses NFTs as both medium and marketplace, extending his practice beyond galleries into global, participatory platforms.

Through NFTs, Murakami linked his *Superflat* philosophy to the logic of blockchain: both flatten hierarchies—between high and low, real and virtual, unique and reproducible. The pixel became his perfect tool: at once retro, playful, and a signifier of value in the digital economy.

Zhang Huan: *Celestial Burial of an Artist*

Another example of pixel art and NFTs is Zhang Huan (b. 1965, China) a famous contemporary artists from China, known for his powerful performances and sculptures. Early in his career he used his own body in extreme works. In *My New York* (2002), for example, he walked through the city wearing a suit made of raw meat, a reference to Tibetan sky burials and the cycle of death and rebirth.

In 2021 Zhang entered the digital world with *Celestial Burial of an Artist*, his first NFT project. Here, he transformed the ritual of sky burial into a virtual and interactive experience. Visitors entered a digital game-like space where Zhang's avatar appeared wearing a pixelated "meat suit." Each participant could select and remove a part of his digital body and then mint it as an NFT. In total, 2,500 body fragments were created. Later, all these pieces were recombined into a large digital artwork.

The project turns pixels into symbols of life, death, and rebirth. Instead of using pixels only for nostalgia or gaming references, Zhang uses them as spiritual building blocks. His work shows how NFTs and digital art can carry deep cultural and ritual meaning, connecting ancient traditions with the newest technology.

Pak's *The Pixel*

One of the most striking examples of the pixel's transformation into a commodity came in 2021 with Pak's NFT artwork *The Pixel*. The piece consisted of nothing more than a single grey pixel, yet it sold for over $1.3 million at Sotheby's. By isolating the most minimal unit of digital imagery, Pak turned the pixel into a symbol of both scarcity and speculation in the NFT boom.

The work raised questions: Was the value in the artwork itself, or in its status as a tradable token? *The Pixel* highlighted how digital culture had entered a new economy, where meaning and price could be detached from artistic labor and instead tied to market hype.

As the NFT bubble cooled in the following years, *The Pixel* also became a reminder of the volatility of digital art markets. What once was celebrated as the future of art quickly faced skepticism and decline, underscoring the risks of treating cultural symbols—like the pixel—not as creative languages but as speculative assets.

Chapter 9 – The Pixel Today: Subculture and the AI Horizon

Pixel art has come a long way from its early days on cathode ray screens. Once dismissed as a limitation of outdated technology, it has now become a thriving global subculture. Artists, game designers, and hobbyists across the world treat the pixel not only as a unit of digital imagery but also as a cultural symbol and artistic medium. Today, pixels live on in online communities, collaborative platforms, museum exhibitions, and even public festivals, while also facing new challenges and opportunities with the rise of generative AI.

In an era dominated by high-definition graphics and photorealistic visuals, pixel art stands out as a deliberate aesthetic choice. Its simplicity, abstraction, and grid-based logic provide a stark contrast to hyper-realistic imagery, inviting audiences to engage imaginatively and interpretively.

eBoy and Paul Robertson

eBoy and Paul Robertson have each played a central role in bringing pixel art into broader public awareness, though in distinct ways. eBoy, a Berlin-based collective, popularized pixel art through meticulously crafted isometric cityscapes and vibrant pop-culture collages, translating urban and commercial imagery into grids that emphasized precision and playful detail. Their work helped legitimize pixel art as a form of mainstream digital and commercial art, inspiring designers and artists worldwide.

Paul Robertson, by contrast, brought pixel art into motion. His densely animated, frenetic style, showcased in projects like *Scott Pilgrim vs. The World: The Game* and viral GIFs, emphasized humor, narrative, and kinetic energy. Robertson demonstrated that pixel art could convey complex stories and emotions, merging retro aesthetics with contemporary pop culture.

Together, eBoy and Robertson illustrate how pixel art evolved from nostalgic graphics into a versatile medium, capable of both static, intricate compositions and dynamic, expressive animation, helping define the genre's contemporary relevance.

Amateur and Professional Pixel Art Communities

The internet has played a pivotal role in the proliferation of pixel art. Platforms like PixelJoint, DeviantArt, and Wplace host thousands of creators, from hobbyists experimenting with retro game aesthetics to professionals designing for commercial projects.

Wplace is a large-scale, collaborative pixel art platform where thousands of users contribute to a single, massive canvas. Each participant can place individual pixels, creating images, patterns, and messages that gradually build into a sprawling, ever-evolving digital artwork. Unlike traditional solo pixel art, Wplace emphasizes collective creativity: no single artist controls the final composition, and each contribution interacts with countless others in real time. It serves as both a social experiment and a digital gallery, demonstrating how community-driven art can flourish in an online environment. The resulting works are unpredictable, chaotic, and dynamic, reflecting the diversity of styles, ideas, and cultural references contributed by participants.

Generative AI and Pixel Art

What about the future of Pixel Art in the age of Generative AI? AI introduces both opportunities and challenges. Tools such as DALL·E and MidJourney can produce pixelated imagery rapidly, assisting artists with prototyping and concept generation. However, AI-generated art also raises questions about authorship, originality, and the value of handcrafted labor.

Some pixel artists embrace AI as a collaborative tool, integrating it into their workflow. Others maintain traditional methods—drawing by hand or coding manually—to preserve the tactile, personal qualities that define the medium. Offline hybrids, like embroidered pixel mosaics, also gain renewed significance as a human-centered response to automated perfection.

The Future of Pixel Art

The future of pixel art will likely be shaped by this interplay between human and machine. Handcrafted pixel art remains celebrated for its precision, personal narrative, and imperfections, while AI introduces new possibilities for scale, variation, and collaborative experimentation. Artists are negotiating these changes in diverse ways: some integrate AI selectively, others use it to push creative boundaries, and many continue to assert the enduring importance of manual craftsmanship.

Overall, pixel art is positioned at a crossroads. Its charm and cultural resonance endure because it balances simplicity, nostalgia, and expressive depth. Whether created by hand or guided by AI, pixels continue to captivate, reminding us that even in a world of perfect, generated graphics, the human eye, mind, and hand remain central to the art form's vitality.

www.ingramcontent.com/pod-product-compliance
Lightning Source LLC
Chambersburg PA
CBHW050026230526
45470CB00003B/1144